Ana Alcaraz

One day, Ricky and his parents were strolling and enjoying a day of celebration in the United States. There were fireworks and people were having a party

Suddenly, while walking past a bookstore, they saw an elderly man encircled by a group of very attentive children

"Dear children, I am going to tell you the story of our land and why people are celebrating it in the streets."

Once upon a time, there was a country called America, where its brave and dreamy inhabitants, known as Colonists, lived under the rule of a king named George

This king belonged to a distant country called England, and he wasn't always fair to them.

Some colonists began to dream of their freedom and believed that all inhabitants of America should have rights and not be governed by a king who lived so far away from their land

They met in a city called Philadelphia to make a plan. They wrote a letter to say they wanted to be free and live their lives the way they wanted, without a king telling them what to do

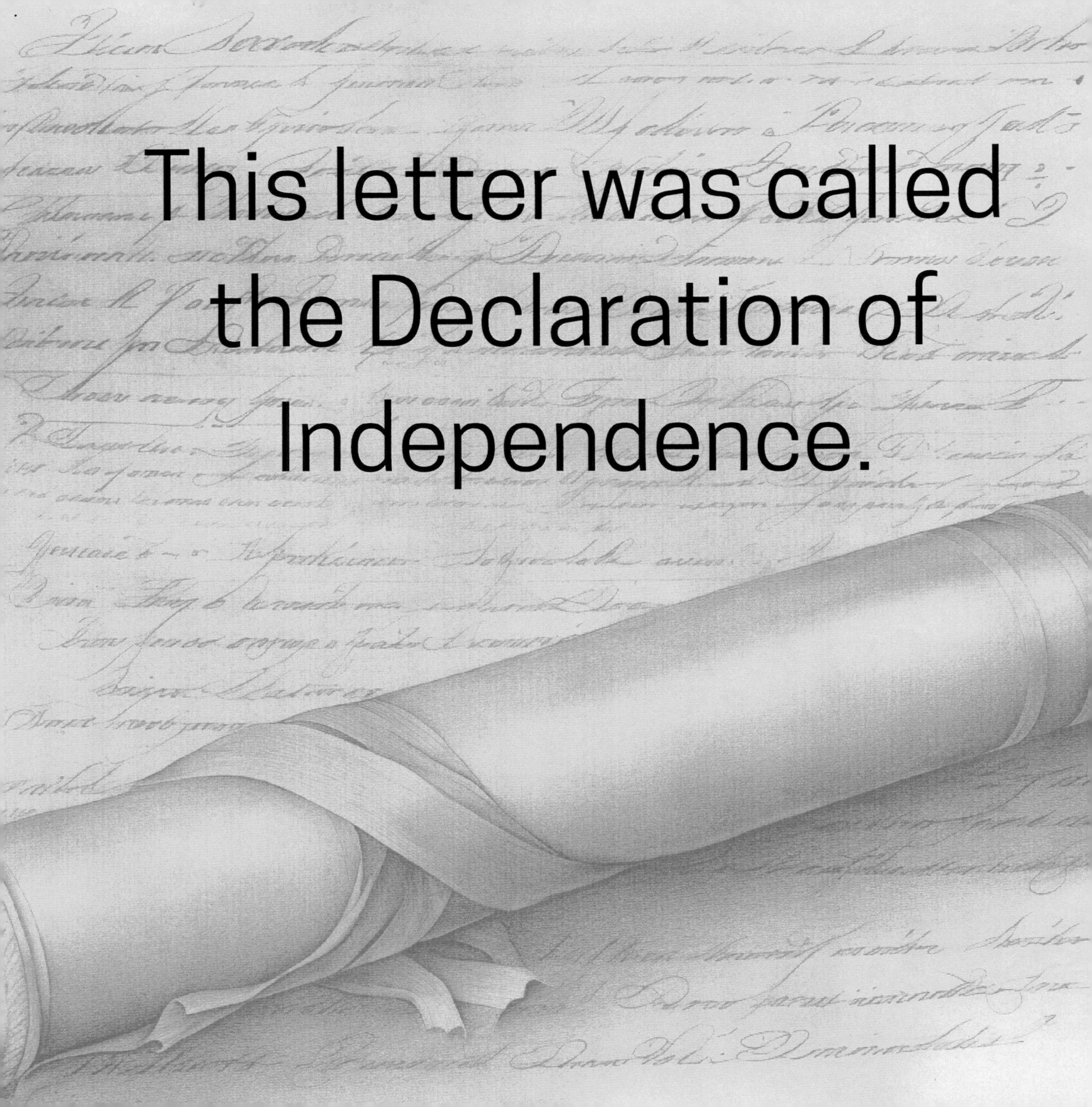

This letter was called the Declaration of Independence.

King George and his government were not pleased with this declaration.
They decided to send an army to America to fight against the rebellion and maintain their control over the land

But the brave inhabitants of America were not scared, and they joined together to form their own army, led by the courageous General George Washington

The war for independence began. The patriots fought with all their might against the powerful army of the king. Despite the difficulties and challenges, they never lost hope nor their desire to be free

After a long time of fighting, the colonists won a big battle called the Battle of Yorktown. The king's army gave up, and America got its independence. It became a free country, and the people who lived there could make their own rules and decisions

All the people celebrated with joy and gratitude on that day. They started building a new country based on the principles of freedom, equality, and justice for everyone.

That's how the United States of America came to be, a special place where dreams can come true. In this land, every person has a chance to be happy and find their own path to success

And since then, every year on Independence Day, which is celebrated on July 4th, the citizens of the United States honor the bravery of those patriotic soldiers who fought for their freedom

The Day of Independence, on July 4th, reminds us that freedom and independence are like treasures that we must always take care of and value. They are very important rights that allow us to be who we want to be and do what makes us happy. We should protect and appreciate them at all times.

And that, dear children, is the story of the independence of the United States, a tale of bravery, hope, and the fight for freedom.

Ricky was so excited when he left the bookstore that he ran to his parents and told them he needed to get a flag quickly. He wanted to join the celebration with everyone!